STOLEN
LIVES

The heart breaking
story of a
trafficking victim

BRANDY SULLIVAN

BRANDY SULLIVAN

Stolen Lives: The Heart Breaking Story of a Trafficking Victim

First Edition

November 2013

Copyright © 2013 Brandy Sullivan

ISBN-13: 978-1492767046

ISBN-10: 1492767042

BRANDY SULLIVAN

If you are or know someone who is a victim of trafficking please call 1-888-373-7888 or text to **BeFree (233733)**

BRANDY SULLIVAN

DEDICATION

Isabelle, with love.

STOLEN
LIVES

The heart breaking
story of a
trafficking victim

BRANDY SULLIVAN

AUTHOR'S NOTE

This book is inspired by real life stories of trafficking victims, however much of what is written is a fictionalized account based on research and anonymous communications with victims who not only found the willpower and strength to escape, but overcame their fears to share their stories with the world. Sharing their stories will help bring awareness to the world and hopefully this awareness will lead to a better understanding of not only the victims but also their captors. Understanding is the first step in infiltrating this underground world and hopefully one day finding a solution to a crime that has become an epidemic worldwide.

BRANDY SULLIVAN

PROLOGUE

Mark sat staring at the bundle of dingy paper, the corners were ripped and the rubber bands holding it together were almost at their breaking point. He sat down with the intention of looking at its contents countless times in the last few days, but until this morning he couldn't bring himself to do it. Flash backs of the girl's pleading blue eyes had haunted his visions since their encounter three days before. The day had been overcast, but muggy as hell. He had just stepped out of Starbucks with his iced latte in hand when she shoved the papers into his chest.

"Please mister, please take these with you. I need your help. Take them and hide them." She whispered quickly, her eyes willing him to cooperate. He almost shoved them back at her, but it was something in those eyes that stopped him. He could see desperation buried in them.

"Um, okay ma'am, but where should I hide them?"

"It doesn't matter, just somewhere safe. If I am not back here in three days, at this same time, it is because something happened to me. If you don't see me here, turn these in to the Miami police department right away." She wasn't looking at him anymore; she was glancing over her shoulder, watching the door of the hotel across the street.

"Shouldn't you just bring them there now if this is a legal matter?" He was noticing the dark bruises on her arms, the sunken cheeks, and her dingy clothing. She wore a pair of blue jeans and a tank top that was probably once a pale blue, but now resembled a gray sky on a stormy morning. On her feet were flip flops that showcased polished toe nails that were broken and jagged. The purple paint had chipped away in spots. Mark was beginning to think maybe she was in an abusive relationship.

"No, you must wait. Please I need your help. I have to go now. I have been gone to long already. Be here in three days please. Promise me!" She pleaded as she took one last deep look into his eyes.

"I promise." He whispered before she fled into the oncoming traffic, focused only on the door to the hotel looming across from them.

Mark had gone back to Starbucks on the promised morning. He sat at one of the tables outside for over three hours. The girl with the desperate blue eyes never appeared. He slowly made his way home, he set the pile of papers on the table and stared at it. He felt nervous and afraid, he knew she wanted him to bring the papers to the police department, but he also knew he needed to know what was in them. He didn't want to turn them in without having read them, inadvertently getting himself involved in something he may not want to be involved in.

Mark's hands were shaking as he began to pull the rubber bands away from the papers. One of them snapped, leaving an angry welt on his finger. The top two pages were blank. He flipped them over and his eyes were bombarded with words scrawled pencil. The words looked hurried, and there were watermarks blurring the lines. Thinking back to the girl he could only assume the watermarks were tear stains. Pushing his chair back from the table he got up and made his way to the fridge. He grabbed a Pepsi and his cigarettes and lighter from on top. As a general rule he didn't smoke inside his house, but the bundle of nerves inside him told him it was okay to break those rules today.

Armed with two vices, caffeine and nicotine, he sat down and began to read the story that would never leave him. Mark had no way of knowing that the girl with the blue eyes would haunt his dreams for the rest of his life.

BRANDY SULLIVAN

I DIDN'T MEAN TO LEAVE YOU

I'm sorry. I'm so so sorry. I know that everybody back home is probably scared and angry. They don't know where I am and I know now they will never find me. As long as I behave they will be safe. At least I can do that for them. Whatever happens I hope one day my mom will see this and know how much I love her and that I will always carry her with me. Mom if you are reading this, I never meant to cause you so much pain. I hope one day we can be together again but that hope scares me. That hope makes me act out and when I act out he punishes me. Maybe I should just put that hope away.

I remember being so excited about going out and getting a job when I turned 16 last summer. I couldn't wait to be independent, couldn't wait for some of my rules to go away, I couldn't wait to be an adult. I took the job at the mall because I liked the attention and I liked meeting all the new and exciting people. I used to complain about the older woman who came to my booth day after day always wanting a free makeover but never buying anything. I swear if I was still working there now I would not complain anymore.

Growing up in Maple Heights made me long for a life in the city. I understand now why we were never allowed to venture to Cleveland and hang out by ourselves. I used to get so jealous when my friends would come to school bragging about parties and clubs they went to in the city. I think that's why I was so excited about the job at the mall. It was a legitimate reason for me to go to the city by myself and I was so jaded. I thought working in the city and being exposed all those people was going to open up a world of opportunities for me. I dreamt of a busy life, a successful career, and a datebook filled with social appointments.

Working at the mall did expose me to lots of people, after all that's how I met Moses. It was a Saturday. I was scheduled to work from eight in the morning until 2 o'clock that afternoon. The mall was busy that day, as it always is on Saturdays. I had hardly gone five minutes without somebody at the booth all day. My cell phone was filling up with text messages from my friends. For many of them the most important thing on a Saturday was to figure out what we were going to do that night.

Moses came to the booth with a younger woman. He said it was his niece who was visiting from out of town. His dark brown eyes were very intense as he explained that she was having a sweet 16 party that night and he wanted her to look pretty. Moses was dressed like he had just stepped off a magazine cover. His slacks perfectly pressed, and his striped button up shirt open at the neck. I could feel the butterflies in my stomach. They always fluttered around when someone handsome talked to me. Stupid butterflies.

"I've sunk so much money into the party already that I can't afford to take her to the salon. I saw you and was hoping a pretty girl like you would understand how important it is to look good on your 16th birthday. You are about 16 aren't you?" He said to me as those brown eyes looked me over from head to toe.

"Yeah I'm 16, I turned 16 a few months ago. I certainly understand wanting to look good for your own party." I blushed at him, welcoming the compliment.

"So you'll give her one of your free makeovers and make her look all grown up?"

"Of course, if she can just hop up on one of the stools we can get started."

I assumed the girl was just really shy. The

whole time I was talking with Moses she never looked up from the floor. She just stood there silent. Moses grabbed her elbow and turned her body towards the stool.

"Hop on up there and hold still, we want you looking your best tonight." He instructed her.

As she climbed up on the stool she finally lifted her head and looked at me. I remember thinking it was odd that a girl about to have her sweet 16 party would look so sad. It was, after all, the biggest day of your teenage life. Her eyes were a steely gray color, and the dark circles underneath told me she hadn't slept very well. I remember not sleeping very well before my 16th birthday. All of the excitement made it hard for me to fall asleep, and reminded me of being little and not being able to sleep on Christmas Eve. I assumed that she was having the same problem.

"Hi, I'm Annabel. What kind of colors were you thinking? I think some nice warm shades would brighten up your face a bit. What do you think?"

"Well... umm... Whatever uncle Moses thinks will look best." She whispered eyes downcast to the floor again.

"Just make her look good, mature...but not old. Kind of sexy." He told me.

I must have given him a funny look when he said the word sexy. Normally uncles don't use that word when referring to their nieces.

"Well you know, I figure girls want to look back at the pictures and think they looked appealing. I mean girls are boy crazy at 16 aren't they? I bet you got loads of boyfriends Annabel, being so pretty and all." He quickly explained.

"Well, I wouldn't say loads." I was blushing again. I started picking out colors for her and realized I still didn't know her name. "I'm sorry, I didn't catch your name." I said to her, but Moses answered for her.

"Tracy, her name is Tracy."

"Well it is very nice to meet you Tracy and happy birthday!" I tried to draw her into conversation with no success.

"Tracy is coming out to Los Angeles with me after her party and is nervous about her new modeling job." Moses explained. "Right Tracy?"

"Um, yeah. It is a bit scary." She mumbled.

"Modeling? Wow, you are so lucky! I would love to have a career like that!" I exclaimed as I applied concealer to her circles. I really wanted her to look her best for her party. Normally when we gave out free makeovers we scrimped on some of the product, but I was treating Tracy like a paying client.

"Yeah I guess." She said, shrugging her shoulders.

"Come now, don't be so worried Tracy. You are going to do great! I just know it." Moses replied, putting a protective hand on her back.

"I am sure you will." I told her, wishing she would cheer up. I was carefully lining her eyes, trying to make them pop.

Moses leaned in to inspect my work. "You do really good at that, she looks amazing. I have an idea and a proposition for you Annabel. Why don't you come to Tracy's party tonight? Some of the scouts from LA will be there. Personally I think you are pretty enough to model for us, but hey if they don't like you for pictures I bet we could use you to do make-up at the shoots. You could understudy one of our regular girls for a bit."

"Me model? I don't know about that. Plus there is no way my mother would let me go to LA."

"So come to the party, don't tell her where you are going or about the offer until after the party. Wait to hear what the scouts have to say before making waves with your mother. If they offer you a contract I bet she would let you. Think of all the college money you could earn."

His reasoning sounded good and I was excited. I had him scribble down the address of the party on the back of one my booth's business cards and promised I would go. Tracy barely smiled at me as she climbed down off the stool. Looking back I think she may have tried to warn me with her eyes but I was too excited to pay attention.

I had no way of knowing what was to come. I remember going home, I remember lying about where I was going, and I remember feeling like I was on top of the world. I did not know my whole world was about to come to a screeching a halt. Getting ready to leave that night I tried to dress grown up and appealing. I wanted to land the job and somehow justify lying to everyone about where I had been. I wanted to be someone important, but most of all I wanted to make everyone proud of me. I took the bus most of the way to the address Moses had instructed me to go to. I walked the last few blocks trying to calm my nerves. I was such a child then, thinking I was walking to my big break, trying to calm the butterflies in my stomach.

I thought I had the wrong address at first and almost turned around. Sometimes when I dream about that day, I dream that I did turn around and that none of this had ever happened. The address was a white house, a ranch style house, only one story. There was a for sale sign in the front yard with a website listed. The bottom of the sign instructed interested buyers to visit the site and leave their contact details. There was only one van in the yard. It was one of those work vans with windows only in the front. It was burgundy and covered in road dust. I stared at it for a few moments before ascending the walkway and meekly rapping on the door. My brain registered the silence permeating from the house, but my immature excitement quieted any doubts my brain was sending me. The door opened a few inches in response to my knock, but it was dark inside the house and I couldn't see who opened it.

"Excuse me, I am sorry to bother you. I was given this address..." I started to explain when Moses poked his head out the door.

"Anna dear!" He proclaimed. "You don't mind if I call you Anna do you? Come in, come in. Tracy is upstairs being indecisive about her hair. Maybe you could give her a hand?" Moses asked, opening the door wider for me to step through.
"I thought there was a party, where is everybody?" I hesitated at the door step, my feet starting to have the same doubts as my brain.

"Oh, the limo will be here in less than fifteen

minutes to take us to the hotel. You didn't think the party was here did you? I am sorry, I thought I explained. I am selling this house; the movers have already emptied most of the furniture. We rented a ballroom for the event, and well the limo is on its way and Tracy could really use some girl-to-girl advice about her hair."

Feeling less nervous and ignoring any alarm bells that had started ringing, I willed my feet to move and crossed the threshold. "Of course, I would be glad to help."

The house was bare, and dark. None of the lights were on and most of the blinds were drawn shut.

"She is up the stairs just ahead, last room on the right." Moses instructed me.

He followed behind me as I took each stair slowly, the doubt was returning with a vengeance. Maybe I could have run then, maybe I could have escaped before it was too late, but I didn't.

BRANDY SULLIVAN

TOO LATE

By the time I reached the top of the stairs I had sealed my fate. The hallway was narrow, the walls stark white, and the floor covered in cheap blue carpet. By the time I was halfway down the hallway I could feel Moses inches behind me. He was following me closely.

"Just right down here, I know Tracy will be so glad to have you here to help her."

"I'm... I mean... I'm just glad I can help." I stammered. I reached out and grabbed the doorknob and as I turned it to open the door I felt Moses, his hand clamped down on my shoulder.

"Right through here dear." He said as he pushed me into a darkened room.

I heard the door slam behind us as

somebody flicked on a small lamp. I began to scream as my brain registered what I was seeing. Moses clamped the violent hand over my mouth.

"If you know what's good for you, you will shut your mouth right now."

The first thing I noticed were the two other men standing in the corner. They were both staring at me, with smirks on their faces, and their stances telling me they were ready to pounce if I made a move. The lamp they had turned on was just a tiny thing, with no shade, sitting on the floor plugged into a wall outlet. Also on the floor was Tracy. She wore nothing but a pair of black thongs and was curled up in the fetal position. She glanced at me quickly before closing her eyes. Moses still had his hand around my mouth, while his other arm was wrapped around my torso pinning me to him. One of the men from the corner approached me. He eyed me up and down before reaching out and grabbing one of my breasts. He squeezed it like a vice, the pain bringing tears to my eyes.

"Well Moses, I have to say you did just fine. I think this one can turn a nice profit." The man grumbled. His breath stunk of coffee and cigarettes. His dark eyes bored into me and scared me more than anyone can imagine. "Moses is going to remove his hand from your mouth, but you are not going to scream. Nod if you understand me."

The tears began to flow from my eyes. I nodded, afraid of making them mad. The word profit was flashing over and over in my head, a big neon sign telling me this wasn't going to be an assault I would be able to return home from. Rumors of kidnapping, prostitution, and sex slavery began to swirl in my head. I hadn't made the connection yet. They were there in my mind, swirling around, but not quite coming together. Moses did remove his hand, but within seconds he was binding my hands behind my back. The man in front of me removed a pair of scissors from his back pocket and held them in front of my face.

"I am going to remove your clothes, make a sound and I will cut you. Nod again if you understand."

I was shaking and my legs began to wobble. They were unsure if they wanted to hold me up anymore. Moses gripped my bound hands and as much as his touch made me cringe I was grateful for support. I had no faith in my legs anymore. I stared at the ceiling as the man snipped my blouse and skirt down the front. He stood back and admired his handiwork as my skirt fell to the floor and my shirt hung wide open, baring my body clad in only my bra and underwear. I mentally kicked myself for wearing my date night underwear. Not that it had seen much use; my dates consisted of mild petting and sloppy kissing in the back seat of a car at most. The sound of Tracy whimpering in the corner reminded me she was there. The other man gave her a rough kick making her cry out.

"Shut up!" he commanded her.

"She is perfect." Moses stated from behind me. "Just what we needed, I told you we find another one Randall."

Randall was the man in front of me. He grunted a response, perhaps in agreement and grabbed my chin in his hand.

"You experienced? Have any boyfriends? You know how to please a man?" He asked me.

I didn't answer him. I couldn't. My mind was in full panic mode and my tongue felt like dead weight in my mouth. He squeezed my chin harder.

"Answer me, don't ever make me ask you something twice." He barked at me.

"Na...no...I mean yes. I had a boyfriend, but that was it." I sobbed. He lightened the pressure on my chin.

"A boyfriend, well I'll be. Looky here Moses we got a real experienced girl on our hands." He was laughing, mocking me. "I am going to check out the goods now, just relax, you might enjoy this."

"Please, please don't....Just let me go. I won't tell anyone...I promise." I stammered at him. Randall and Moses both laughed out loud in response. I knew with full certainty listening to those laughs that I was doomed. Using the scissors Randall cut away my bra and underwear. They were both making crude comments about my body, but I tuned them out. I tried to focus on a spot on the wall, reciting song lyrics in my head. I couldn't take it. My mind couldn't take it. My own brain was betraying me and retreating deep inside itself. I felt rough hands on my body, touching, pinching, and squeezing. My tears had stopped flowing, there were none left in me, but my body continued to tremble. I was forced down onto my knees while Moses held me by the hair. Randall had undone his pants and wanted me to show him just how experienced I was. I cried, and pleaded with him not to make me. My pleas were answered with a slap across the face. My head was ringing and I felt a trickle of blood leak from my nose. What followed were perhaps the worst hours of my life. I have had worse happen since then, but I was so naïve. Those hours stripped me of my childhood, my dreams, and any life I had.

At some point, mercifully I had passed out. I awoke still bound and nude on the floor next to Tracy. She was sitting up now and rubbing my hair, brushing strands out of my face that had stuck to my tears and blood.

"Shhh, just rest. You will be okay. I know it doesn't seem like it but you will. Just rest now." She whispered.

Trying to sit up, but finding my body uncooperative I looked at her from the floor "Rest? We need to figure out a way out of here. Help me undo my hands. Maybe we can sneak out while no one is in here."
"Anna, we can't and you must not try to. They will kill you. There is no escape. They own you now, just as they own me. You will get used to it. It takes some time, but the better you behave, the better they will treat you."

"Behave? Are you insane?!" I yelled at her. "Did you see what they did to me? They need to be in jail, we need to get out of here."

"Anna, they won't go to jail. They are too smart for that. You don't understand, but you will."

The magnitude of what she was saying began to sink in, as the tendrils of thoughts from earlier began to connect. I was going to be one of those lost girls on the missing children posters, my family would search for me but no one would find me. Eventually they would all think I was dead somewhere. Eventually they would forget about me.

20

"Tracy, how can you just sit here? Why are you so calm?"

"Well for me this is my home, well not here, but with Moses. Moses rescued me...now don't say anything just listen," she said when she heard me gasp. How could she think this man rescued her?

"My father used to beat me and my mother ran out on us after she got sick of him beating her. When she left he turned to me for all his needs, all of them. Eventually I got up the nerve to run away. I had big plans. I was going to go to Hollywood and be a star. How stupid I was. I ended up hitching from Dallas to Santa Fe. That is when Moses found me. I had to do things for most of the rides I got. Old men with wives at home get lonely on the road."

Tracy went silent for a moment, probably remembering her ordeal. I didn't say anything, mostly because I didn't know what to say. I was appalled and didn't understand any of it. Why didn't she seek legal help when her dad treated her that way? After a few moments she went on.

"The last man I got a ride from smelled awful. He let me in his truck without asking for anything and when we neared Santa Fe he decided to make his move. He wanted payment for the ride after all. I tried to tell him no, but he wasn't having it. He raped me, beat me, and raped me some more. I didn't even think I would be able to walk after. He left me with a few dollars for the shower at the truck stop and spat on me as he shoved me out of his truck. Moses found me crumpled on a bench. He took me in, fed me, clothed me, and put me to work. Because I behaved and made no attempts at running he turned me into his bottom."

"What's a bottom?" I asked.

"Well in exchange for keeping an eye on the other girls I get some freedoms. He takes me shopping sometimes and I never go hungry. Plus he tries to only let the better costumers have me. This should be your goal. The better you behave, the more money you make them, the nicer this will be for you"

"Nicer? How is any of this nice? We are prisoners, slaves! Don't you get it?!" I asked incredulous to her way of thinking. She was a brainwashed robot.

"No see, Moses will let me go when I am done earning my way out. When that day comes he will set me up with a nice bank account and my own house. I will never need a man for anything when that happens."

"Tracy if that is what he promised you I cannot for one second believe that you fell for it."

"You will see it will happen. Hopefully sooner if you behave and do things right, you might replace me. You could be my ticket out. Now I am going to take a nap, I suggest you do the same. We have a long night ahead of us."

She rolled over away from me and went to sleep. Her statement about a long night made my stomach lurch. There was no way I was going to be able to fall asleep.

BRANDY SULLIVAN

BROKEN

As I laid there listening to Tracy snore I tried to tell myself someone would come looking for me. A little voice in my head kept reminding me that I had told no one where I was going. No one knew about Moses, the party, or the address. My hands ached from the bindings and my body was sore from the violent invasion. Tears trickled from my eyes off and on. Anger began to build inside me with the sadness and despair. If I ever got the chance I would kill them, I vowed to myself. I could tell by the shadows of the blinds that it was completely dark out by now. I could hear people moving around on the floor below us. No matter how hard I tried to wiggle my hands and free myself nothing worked.

"Would you quit it, I am trying to sleep!" Tracy snapped at me when my escape efforts woke her up.

"I am so sorry that my will to escape this nightmare is bothering you." I snapped back at her.

She sat up and glared at me. "Listen, you need to curb that attitude right now. I wouldn't want to see something bad happen to you."

"Something bad?! You mean worse than what already happened? I'd say something bad already happened to me." I snapped at her.

"That wasn't bad, actually they were pretty gentle. You are very attractive you know. They probably didn't want to damage the merchandise. Feel lucky. They were just trying to show you what would be expected of you. Think of it as your modeling career, only you model for a select group of costumers." She smirked at me.

I wanted to slap her, if my hands were untied I probably would have. I couldn't believe for one second that this girl, clearly abused, underweight, and nude on the floor with me thought that she had such a good life. They weren't taking care of her. My god, people treated their dogs better than this.

"Hush now and behave." Tracy whispered as we both heard footsteps outside in the hallway. I watched the doorknob turn as I fought my body to keep the bile in my stomach down.

Moses entered the room with a tray of food and a duffel bag slung over his shoulder.

"How is she Tracy?" He asked as he closed the door behind him.

"I want to go, please let me go home." I pleaded.

"Shut the fuck up!" He barked at me. "Unless you want to get hurt, only speak when spoken to."

"She needs to adjust, but she seems healthy enough." Tracy responded. "Feisty attitude though."

"I do not need to adjust!" I cried at them.

Moses set the tray of food down on the floor, dropped the duffel bag beside it and crossed the room in three long strides. Pulling his arm back he slapped me so hard my vision went black for a moment.

"I said to speak when spoken too. Nod if you understand."

The pain was intense; I fought the urge to cry. I didn't want to cry in front of them. Fear of being hit again forced me to nod my head in understanding.

Moses unzipped the duffel bag and pulled

out a brush and hair ties.

"Two braids, make her look young." He instructed Tracy as he handed her the items. I sat there on the floor shivering from shock and fear as she brushed my hair and styled it as instructed.

"Eat." He next instructed her after she finished. She went and sat down in front of the tray of food, gobbling greedily at whatever was on the plate. Moses approached me with a glass of water that had been o the tray.

"Listen closely." He said as he squatted in front of me. "Tonight is your debut. We have to go for a bit of a drive and because you are new you have earned no trust yet. This means there will be special circumstances when we transport you."

He set the glass down and removed two things from his shirt pocket. One was a syringe and one was a pill. He held them both in front of me to examine.

"Now this pill will make you groggy but has no long term side effects. I believe you would know it as a roofie. I can put this in the water and you can drink the entire glass or if you choose not to cooperate I can stick you with this." He said waving the syringe back and forth in front of me. "Trust me you don't want what is in this, but I will use it if need be."

Even with my limited knowledge of street drugs I was afraid of the syringe. I knew that anything in there had to be bad news. I didn't want the roofie either. I didn't want to lose control of my thoughts and body.

"What if I just promise to be good? I wouldn't do anything wrong."

Moses laughed. "Option A or option B. That is it; now make your pick before I stick you with this." He threatened, motioning with the syringe. I reluctantly nodded at the pill and watched him drop it in the glass and swirl the clear liquid around until the pill had dissolved.

"Wise choice." He said moving the glass towards my mouth. "Now open up, I will be nice and help you drink it. Feel special about that. Just ask Tracy, she drank from a bowl on the floor for weeks."

"Yeah I did, but not anymore." She mumbled with a mouthful of food. "Moses takes care of me now."

I parted my lips as he tilted the glass. The water was cool and soothing on my throat as it went down. I didn't know, had no way of knowing, how many hours I had been locked in the room, but I did know I was parched. The effects of the drug were swift. The room began to swirl and everything got fuzzy. A sense of euphoria came over me. Suddenly my mind could not focus long enough for me to even register fear or anger at my situation. It was actually nice to not think about it for a bit. I know that sounds awful but it is true. Moses undid my hands at some point, and I remember a bathroom. He must have taken me to relieve myself. I remember soft fabric being draped on my body, a small nightgown or robe perhaps. When he was done getting me ready he carried me to the van that had been parked in the driveway. At least I think it was that van. I was placed in the back on a bare floor with no seats. Tracy held my head in her lap as she sat leaning against the side of the van. Eventually I slept. I have no idea how long we drove or what direction we went in. There were no windows in the rear of the van and the drugs had taken a strong hold on my senses.

During my drug induced sleep I dreamt of home. My mother and I had gone apple picking. It was early fall and we were in the kitchen peeling apples together to make pies for the family. The sunlight shone through the kitchen windows and kissed my cheeks as I sat at the marble island my father had installed over the summer. Life was normal; there was no danger there, no fear, no pain. We were idly chatting about school and boys when the sunlight changed to darkness. The apple in my hand rotted and turned to mush. When I looked down at it I was horrified to see worms crawling in the brown rotting meat of it. I dropped it and looked up at my mother, searching her face for an explanation. I looked on in horror as the fine lines around her eyes and mouth turned to deep crevices. She aged 10-years in front of my eyes.

"You lied to us Annabel. You lied and you left us. You broke my heart and now they are going to break yours." She croaked as her gray hair began to fall out in clumps and her skin began to sag.

"No mother! I didn't mean it! I promise I didn't mean it! Please stop, please save me!" I pleaded with her.

"I can't save you Annabel, no one can. You left and you broke my heart. I am going to die now because my heart has broken into more pieces than anyone can fix. All your fault. This is all your fault." She whispered through her now labored breathing as she shriveled into nothing before my eyes.

I woke up screaming as Tracy soothed my forehead.

"Everything is okay. It was just a dream." She whispered to me.

Tears stained my face as I sobbed silently into her lap. Nothing was okay and I knew I had broken my mother's heart.

BRANDY SULLIVAN

EVERYONE HAS A PRICE

As far back as I can remember my mother and I had always butted heads. I always thought she was trying to suffocate me when she wouldn't let me do something. Clothes. Clothes were the biggest and most frequent arguments we had. She didn't want me shopping at Victoria secret with my friends. She didn't understand why teenage girls needed those frilly things. My skirts had to be certain lengths and cleavage was taboo in our house. There were days I thought I hated her, days I wanted her to disappear. When she and my father would fight, secretly I always rooted for him to win. It didn't matter what the fight was about. She won all our arguments so I wanted her to see how it felt to be on the losing side now and then.

Less than 24-hours changed my whole outlook on life. Lying in the back of the van, not knowing what life had in store for me I realized what a spoiled, narcissistic child I had been. If I could go back and change things I wouldn't argue, I would say thank you. Thank you for looking out for me, thanking you for trying to instill morals in me, thank you for loving me.

The smooth ride in the van had turned into a bumpy one. We were no longer driving on pavement. The change must have happened while I was lost in my own thoughts.

"Are you awake back there girls?" Moses yelled from the front.

"Yes sir, we are." Tracy replied. She tried to sound happy, but I caught an underlying tone of fear in her voice and felt her body grow tense.

"Good we will be there soon, so be ready."

Sitting up I probed Tracy's face with my eyes, looking for a hint of what was waiting for us.

"Listen Anna, and listen closely. If you follow the rules I give you tonight should go smoothly." She whispered to me.

"Rules? What rules? What is tonight?" I asked feeling nauseous again. The drug had worn off but my head was still a bit dizzy.

"Okay, listen...we are going to what they call an auction night. There will be lots of men and maybe a few women there. When they tell you it is your turn, you hold your head high and try to look as sexy as you can. In my experience the men with more money are better. A bit more classy, well most of them anyway, but I don't want to scare you." She began to explain.

"You mean they are auctioning us off?" I barely choked out as fear strangled me.

"Well for an hour or so, yes. You want to get a good guy to bid on you. Good guys will treat you good, get it?"

"I don't want anyone bidding on me. I won't. I won't do it." My voice was rising with panic.

"Shhh. You don't want Moses to hear you saying that, trust me. Better to be bid on then punished. Some girls don't come back from punishment. Girls that don't cooperate disappear, and none of us are stupid enough to think they get let go and sent home."

The look on her face as she spoke told me she was serious. My imagination began to run away with me. I starting thinking back to news stories and movies I had seen on TV. If any of that stuff was accurate I knew I would end up dead if I didn't cooperate. The van came to a sudden stop as I fought for balance and sanity.

"Let's go girls, and no funny business when I open the door. Anna I will be watching you." Moses stated as I heard him open and close the driver's door, getting out to come around and retrieve us.

Suddenly the van felt safe. Despite its musty smell and cramped quarters I knew I did not want to leave. The trembling returned to my body and although I did not know with 100% certainty what I faced my body thought it had a pretty good idea and went limp on me.

"Out, out now." Moses instructed after he opened the back door to the van. Tracy climbed out, but I was frozen in place.

"I said out!" Losing his patience Moses reached in and grabbed a handful of my hair, painfully yanking me out head first. I collapsed on the ground at his feet.

"Here, let me help you." Tracy reached down and grabbed me by the elbow, helping my wobbling legs stand up and support me.

"I can't...I just can't do this." I sobbed as I stood there. Tears and snot dripping down my face, I was getting hysterical. Panic gripped me. Flashes of dirty men, grunting over me were sweeping through my brain. "Please ... please let me go. I don't deserve this."

"You wanted a job showing off your body,

well here it is." Moses smirked as he grabbed me and tossed me over his shoulder. I tried to struggle, to kick and punch him in the back with my small fists, but the long ride, panic attacks, and lack of food were already making me weak.

Swatting me on the butt Moses just laughed, "Go ahead and fight, some of them prefer it that way. They will fight back, just a word of warning."

Realizing I was not going to get away I hung my head and sobbed as he carried me up a dirt driveway to an old farm house.

There were other cars parked half-hazard about and men standing around smoking cigarettes. Moses walked straight up the front two steps that groaned under our collective weight. Tracy was right behind us, when I peeked up at her she was walking straight as an arrow with eyes downcast at her feet. For someone who said it was all going to be okay she looked scared. The porch had at one time been painted blue, but was now weather worn and dirty gray. Moses said something to the man stationed at the door about the last package arriving. I did not realize that the package he was referring to was me. The man grunted a response and moved out of the way to let us through.

Moses plunked me down hard once we were

inside. I took him less than a minute to grip my arm in his vice-like hands.

"Now behave." He hissed as he led us through the entry way and into the kitchen. There were men playing poker at a small round table in the middle of the room. The linoleum was cracked and peeling, I almost lost my balance stumbling over a piece that was curled up.

"My, my...someone is an eager little slut aren't they?" One of the card men shouted to which they all responded with hearty laughter. I could feel my face burning with embarrassment and rage.

"Fuck you!" I spat at them which only brought another round of laughter and firm shake from Moses who was squeezing my arm so tight, it was sure to bruise.

"You will pay for that you little bitch." He hissed dragging me towards a door across the kitchen.

The door led to a concrete basement. There were 12-stairs leading down. I didn't dare struggle for fear of falling or being shoved down them. No matter how scared I was, self-preservation still reared its head. In the basement there were at least fifteen other girls of varying ages. Some were sitting on thin mattresses on the floor and a few were tied to pipes. Tracy took a seat on one of the mattresses, but I was dragged to the water heater where another man I hadn't noticed tied me with thick rope. I learned later on that the girls who were not tied up had earned the privilege through good behavior. I was new and had earned nothing. Moses left me there without saying word. It may sound strange, but he was the only person I knew and being left with another strange man made me wish he had stayed. The other man looked dirty and cruel.

"You need to be marked." He said to me as his grey eyes looked me up and down with nothing but disgust. He pulled a small branding tool out of his pocket. I didn't realize what it was until he started heating the end of it with his lighter. Once it was hot enough for him he yanked up my nightgown, exposing my bare bottom.

"No! No! Please don't!" I screamed, squirming to keep him from getting a clear shot at my skin.

"Get over here and hold her Lucy." He called to a skinny brunette girl who was sitting on the mattress with Tracy. Without saying a word she got up and approached me, eyes downcast to the floor. As she got closer I gasped realizing she couldn't have been more than 13-years-old. She bear hugged me around the waist, squeezing her eyes shut and ignoring my screams.

The pain was quick and intense as the man found his target with the hot metal. I could feel it sinking into my skin as the smell of burning flesh hit my nostrils. The girl released me as he pulled the tool away. I was sobbing uncontrollably. He had branded me with an M, for Moses I assumed.

"Now we know who you belong to, in case for some reason your pretty face in unrecognizable at the end of the night." He chuckled, giving me freshly seared skin a slap before pulling my night gown back down.

Glancing at his watch, he addressed the room, "Okay ladies! Showtime!"

On his cue the cellar door opened and a small group of men, led by Moses were brought down the stairs. Each man took his time eyeballing us before conferring with Moses over price. It was an old man, with white balding hair and a large pot belly protruding over his dark blue trousers who apparently bid on me. I watched in horror as he paid Moses and came over to retrieve me.

"Well hello sweet heart." He rasped as he untied me from the water leaving, leaving the knots that bound my wrists intact. "You and me are going to have loads of fun. Let's go!" He jerked on my bound hands and dragged me behind him.

We went back up the stairs and through another door off the kitchen into a sparsely furnished room. He threw me onto the bed that felt crusty and stunk of acts I didn't want to think about. I lay there trembling, unsure of what to do. My eyes darted around the room as I frantically tried to figure out a way out of the room, away from the sweating man who was stripping off his clothes.

"Don't be afraid." He breathed, his erection already evident.

"Listen, this is some mistake. I'm...I'm not a prostitute." I tried to reason with him as he approached me.

Laughing he grabbed his erection and waved it back and forth. "Oh I know you're not. You're a beautiful little tramp who needs what I have."

He grabbed my ankle, straightening me out on the bed, climbing over me. His eyes were wild with lust as I struggled beneath his sweating pudgy body.

"No! Get off me! Get the hell off me!" I screamed as he tried to force my legs open with his own. He clamped his hand over my mouth and forced himself inside me. It hurt, the more I struggled the worse it hurt. All I could think about was getting away from him, when his hand slid down my mouth from the force of his thrusts I bit down as hard as I could. I tasted blood as it trickled into my mouth. To my surprise he didn't climb off me. He punched me instead. Pain exploded in my face as I felt blood gush out of my nose. I was nothing to him but something to be used and discarded. I gave up all fight and just lay there, trying to escape somewhere inside my mind, somewhere where things were still safe.

That night was my first real night earning my keep as Moses put it. I didn't struggle with anyone after that. My nose was broken and I was covered in blood and filth from the men who came to the room. Moses did feed me at the end of the night. A peanut butter sandwich and a glass of water. Even with all I had been through, I was starving. I hadn't eaten since before leaving work and the sun was coming up. I had survived my first day as a captive, well my body had survived, something broke inside me...my soul, my spirit, whatever you want to call it. I lost my ability to hope and dream.

MARK

Mark's chair scraped across the floor and fell with a loud bang as he jumped back from the table. He ran to the sink feeling nauseous, but all he could do was dry heave. Was all of this real? He just couldn't believe what he was reading. His head was spinning; he didn't know what to do. His first instinct was to run to the phone and call the police, but a nagging voice in his head that wouldn't shut up and was repeatedly asking him if this was something he really wanted to get involved in stopped him. With a shaky hand he grabbed a glass out of the cupboard and filled it with cold tap water. He took a couple of sips and felt his stomach begin to settle.

Deep down he knew he should call the police; he kept glancing back towards the table at the pile of papers, as much as the words written on them terrified him he wanted to know more. He was suddenly concerned for the girl's well-being and wanted to know how everything turned out. He started telling himself that if she was able to sneak in the stack of papers that she must have some sort of freedom, she'd probably escaped by now and that's why she didn't show up for their meeting. Maybe he shouldn't call the police after all. If she did manage to get free, he would be sending them on a wild goose chase, he reasoned to himself. Mark walked around the table a few times trying to calm his nerves. His conscience told him the weather here escaped or not the police still needed to know. He realized he may be her only hope of escape or rescue.

"Out of all the people on earth, why? Why did it have to be me? Why did I have to go to Starbucks that morning?" He said to the empty kitchen.

Mark had seen movies about people being stolen and used as slaves, but he didn't really believe that stuff happened right here in The United States. Those things happened in third world countries, with corrupt government agencies and parents who sold their kids to make a quick buck. This had to be a joke, or a woman who was unhappy in her marriage, maybe a scorned step-daughter. The girl looked frightened though. Those eyes, the desperation that seeped from them flashed through his mind. Something was happening to her, that or she was a damn good actress.

Mark shuffled the papers back into a neat pile as he decided what he was going to do. Grabbing his keys off the kitchen counter he took the pile and fled to his car. While driving to Kinkos he couldn't help but scan the faces of the girls adorning the sidewalks. He was hoping one was Anna, but he also knew that was highly unlikely given her situation. Pulling into Kinkos he parked his car as close to the entrance as he could. He was grateful when he scanned the parking lot and found it was all but deserted. He didn't want nosey eyes prodding his documents as he ran copies. It took him a half an hour and all the ones in his billfold to make a complete duplicate of the diary. The diary that no longer seemed just a pile of dingy paper to him, but a life line to Anna.

Mark stopped at the first police department he came to, it wasn't his local precinct. He had driven across town to Kinkos and now he was hoping no one would recognize him as he dropped off his burden. Approaching the front counter he set the pile of papers down and cleared his throat to get the woman's attention who was busy shuffling papers and signing forms.

"Could you see that a detective or somebody gets this please, it's important." He stated when she looked up at him. Before she even got a word out in response Mark turned to leave.

"Sir, sir? If you could wait just a minute..." Her voice faded away as Mark rushed out the glass doors to his waiting car on the street. He felt a sense of relief as he sped towards home, with his copy of the diary safely on the passenger seat.

Arriving home Mark opted for the solace of his office on the second floor to read more about Anna's fate. He felt a connection to her; she was a magnet, her story drawing him like a nail to her agonizing life. He could see her face, her eyes burning with pain, as if she was standing in the room with him. With shaky hands he flipped through his copy and found his place, taking a breath he steeled himself for the words that would undoubtedly stay with him, burned into his soul forever.

RESIGNATION

I was crying again, not my normal refined teenage crying, but full on 5-year-old, I just skinned my knee and I think I am going to die crying. I was sobbing and heaving, with snot pouring down my face. I was in a basement of another house; there had been so many houses. There were other girls in the basement with me. None of them were making all the fuss that I was. They didn't look happy, they looked resigned. I wasn't interested in their names or stories; I didn't want to hear them tell everything would be fine. Nothing was fine; nothing would ever be fine again.

This basement had no windows and no mattresses or blankets on the floor. Just dusty, damp concrete. There were 5-gallon buckets in the corners for us to use as toilets in case we got the urge. You wouldn't think that basic human needs would cross your mind in situations like that but they do. They are always there as constant nagging reminders that this is real life, that this is my life. It isn't a dream, it isn't a nightmare, and when your bladder or bowels says its time you can't ignore it. Using the buckets as a place to relieve myself was one more shameful experience that I found a way to endure. For some odd reason it was harder than some of the other, more painful things I had been through. Using a bucket made me feel less than human, almost animal like. Emptying my bladder for others to see, waiting for scraps of food, being kicked and punched when I am naughty, it was all degrading and dehumanizing. We were just captive animals, at the complete mercy of our masters. I think I have been with Moses for two weeks, maybe a bit more. Time has no meaning. I don't count the days, and honestly there is no point. Even if I see the sun rise and set I cannot for certainty that I am waking up to a rising sun the very next morning. The drugs mess with your sense of time. I don't get them every day, only when I become hysterical or they are transporting me.

I knew the other girls were getting annoyed with my blubbering, but I couldn't understand why they weren't crying as well. I made a silent vow to myself to never get used to the life of a slave, I would not act as resigned as they did. The funny thing was though; there was no conviction in that vow. I knew what punishments awaited me if I acted out, and I knew I hadn't seen the worst punishments these men could dole out. I felt as if I was going crazy and I longed to crazy at the same time. Crazy enough to no longer know or care about reality, like people in stories who can get lost within their own minds, never to be seen or heard from again.

"Hey! Hey you, blubber mouth! What are you carrying on about? Whatever it is, it is giving me a head ache!" A plump brunette yelled to me from across the room.

"Nobody's home! Leave a message at the beep." I barked at her, switching from crying to hysterical laughter.

The brunette got up and crossed the room, as she headed towards me I noticed her toenails were painted green and her fingernails were purple. Her black shorts and tank top looked ten times too small for her, excess flesh bulging to escape the tight fabric where ever there was an exit.

"Your polish doesn't match!" I yelled at her as I went on laughing. I couldn't stop. I saw the look on her face, I knew she was not coming to hug me, but I just went on laughing, with tears and snot still dripping down my face.

Her shadow loomed over me as she planted her feet squarely in front of me.

"Shut up! Do you hear me, shut the fuck up. We only get so many minutes of peace and privacy, just shut up and let the rest of us try to relax!" She screamed down at me.

I focused on her legs, her plump stubbly legs.

"Maybe you should shave before you turn into Snuffleupagus!" I giggled out at her. That's what my mother always said to me when I left stubble on my legs and she saw it. I knew I was cracking up, I wanted to crack up, I longed for the sweet bliss of crazy town.

I saw her foot, the green polish a blur, as she brought it towards my face. I didn't really register the movement of the foot accelerating at me until it connected with my chin. My teeth clanged together as the pain set in. I didn't make a move to retaliate, I just let them pain wash over me and wash away my laughter and tears. She stood there staring at me for at least a minute, waiting to see if another kick would be needed to keep me quiet. Satisfied that one was enough she grunted before turning on her heel and walking back to her spot on the basement floor. Once she sat down two girls who had been watching the episode walked over to me and sat down on either side. One was a rather plain looking blonde girl who I guessed was probably no more then 17-years-old. The other was a Chinese girl, well girl isn't the right word, she was a woman. She spoke first.

"Hi my name is Darlene."

"I am sorry if I was bothering you guys as well. I just don't understand how everybody can sit here so calmly as if we are not in the worst possible situation we could be in. I'm Anna by the way."

"Well Anna, for me staying calm is better than pulling my hair out and going nuts. I know this sucks, believe me I know. I feel like I have been doing this forever." Darlene said as she placed a hand on my back in comfort.

"How long have you been held captive?" I inquired.

"I can't say with 100% accuracy, I just know it feels like it's been years and years. My parents brought me to the United States as a child and we obtained citizenship. I met a nice man when I was 17. He was in the Navy and seemed every inch a gentleman. When I turned 18 I eagerly rushed down the aisle with him and we were married. He told me that he owned a house out in the country and that that is where we would live and raise a family. I thought I was the luckiest girl on earth, I couldn't wait to start my life as an adult woman.

I was so stupid. Our first night in his house was like everything out of a romance movie. The next day he transported me to an abandoned house in a remote area of the woods. I had no idea where the house was, I had never been in this part of the country before. It was there that he handcuffed me to an old radiator. I was left there for days while all of his buddies took turns coming visiting. I was raped and beaten continually.

After days of nonstop abuse a middle-aged woman who had been coming by the house and watching what all of the men were doing came up to me. She seemed very nice and concerned for my well-being. She told me that she ran an escort service, and that if I came and worked for her for a period of a few months she could take me away from all of this. I didn't want to be an escort, I mean that's the same as being a prostitute, but I knew I had to get away from where I was or I would end up dead.

After a few weeks of working for her I was well compensated with food, clothing, and anything I could possibly need. At first all of the clients that came just wanted an escort. They didn't ask for sex, they just wanted a date, a beautiful girl on their arm. I thought it was a great arrangement and was honestly happy. I was so jaded. Finally one night one of my clients requested sex. I adamantly refused, but he didn't care. I was grabbed a hold of and thrown on the floor. There he raped and beat me. I was mortified and terror-stricken. I ran to the nearest police station to file a report. The officers just looked at me like I was crazy. They explained to me that I couldn't file a report because I was a prostitute.

The woman who hired me was irate when she found out I had been to the police station. She was now facing a possible investigation. She explained to me that I was too much of a risk for her to keep around, but I still owed her a large debt that I would have to pay off. She explained to me that because of this debt she could not just let me go. It was then that I realized I was her prisoner. She locked me up in a closet for a few days until a man came. Apparently she was selling me to the man to pay off my debt to her, which of course meant I now owed a debt to him.

I spent months being constantly paraded around in front of potential clients. By then I was resigned to my fate, and the most I could hope for was that the client would be nice and treat me with at least a shred of decency. The man who bought me trained me to speak in broken English. Apparently men paid more if they thought I wasn't from the United States.

Over the next two years I was sold to three different men, each one paying off my old debt only to establish a new one. I've been in this area now for about six months. I have learned over the years that if I behave and pretend I enjoy it the punishments and torture are far less. At this point I can endure the sex far better than I can endure the beatings"

I looked at Darlene with resignation and understanding. She was cleaner and better dressed then most us, she didn't have the faded yellow marks of old bruises healing littering her skin. She had found a way to survive in this life, a life that none of us chose, but it was a life none the less.

It was listening to Darlene and seeing the sincerity in her eyes that made me realize I had to choose. This was now my life, and I could live it as comfortable as possible or be beaten until they finally killed me. I know there are people who would never understand, I mean how could they? Unless they are in the same position. I felt the tears well up in my eyes, not hysterical tears this time, but tears of understanding my fate finally and coming to terms with it. I hugged Darlene and thanked her for her words. Because of her I was able to get through the night with minimal pain and no beatings to speak of. Moses was actually happy and allowed me a warm private shower and a hot meal.

TRANSPORTED

I still wasn't sure where I was. The next few weeks passed by as smoothly as they could. I won't even begin to say that they were easy, all I can say is that they were less painful. I now had clean clothes, warm food, and showers whenever I needed them. One night I even got to sit in the living room and watch TV. One of the stations was playing episodes of the Big Bang Theory and for a little while I almost forgot where I was, laughing at some of the more comical parts. That is until a man came bursting in with a flyer in his hand screaming at Moses.

"Have you seen this? They're all over the place, her parents haven't stopped looking for her. I told you to get her out of the area. Sell her to somebody else if you have to."

Getting up from the couch Moses marched over to the man and ripped the flyer out of his hand. He studied it for a minute crumpled it up and threw it across the room.

"Just calm down." He said addressing the man. "It's not like they have any idea where she is, they probably think she ran away from home and is with one of her ex-boyfriends or something."

Somehow I knew they were talking about me, my family was out there searching for me, they still loved me.

"Moses, you could let me go. My parents, well they're not rich, but they could pay you whatever my debt is. I mean we wouldn't have to involve the police or anything."

"You think the flyer is about you." Moses laughed at me. "It's not about you, your parents aren't looking for you, they are probably glad you're gone. You were selfish and you lied to them and now they are probably just happy to not think about you anymore. Now go to the basement."

I had made it through the last few weeks mainly by detaching myself from my old life. The flyer changed everything. I longed for freedom, I longed for my mother to hold me in her arms again, I longed for my bedroom and the silly stuffed animals that covered my bed. I even longed for the pop quizzes in Mrs. Young's algebra class.

Standing up, I crossed my arms over my chest, and spat at Moses "my parents will always love me, they will never stop looking, they will find me. One of these days I will escape, you won't know when and you won't know how, but I will get away."

It took Moses all of 10 seconds to cross the room and backhand me across the face. He then proceeded to kick me in my back and legs while yelling profanities at me the whole time. By the time the vicious beating was over it took me all the energy I had left in my broken body to crawl to the basement and make it down the stairs. My few weeks on easy street were over. I knew it would take me a while to earn back Moses's trust, I was now part of the basement crew again instead of his group of prized girls.

Curled up on the basement floor I tried to pull up images of good memories from home, from my childhood. They all seemed so far away. It's like they were there but I just couldn't get the pictures to come into focus. Everything I tried to imagine came in blurry. I just wanted to see everybody's face again in my mind, one more time before I locked them away in some deep vault within my subconscious where I wouldn't have to think about them anymore.

I wasn't brought out of the basement for work that night; I assumed it was because of the beating I had received. Angry red and purple welts were appearing on my body and there was dried blood on my face. It wasn't until the first morning rays of light were peeking through the dingy window that I found out the real reason.

"Anna! Anna! Get up here right now!" Moses screamed down the basement stairs.

Grimacing in pain I slowly stood up. There are deep aches that accost your body when you have been sleeping on a cold concrete floor, aches I didn't even know were possible. With the help of the iron railing I pulled myself up the stairs and stood with my eyes downcast in front of Moses.

"Jesus Anna, you look like shit. Go clean yourself up. You have ten minutes."

Of course I looked like shit, I wanted to scream at him, you beat me and left me in basement after. I didn't say anything though, I was too sore to ask for more pain. I stumbled to the bathroom and filled the sink with warm water. I stared into the grey-blues in the mirror that looked foreign to me now. I barely recognized myself. I didn't want to recognize myself. Shaking my head I dipped a cloth into the water and began washing the blood away. I sponged bathed all the important areas and finger combed my hair. The fluorescent lighting above the mirror made the ugly bruises look so much worse. There wasn't anything I could do about them and if Moses didn't get good pay for me because of them it was his own fault I thought to myself. I figured I had been in the bathroom maybe 5-minutes, which meant I still had time. I sat on the cold toilet seat trying to relieve anything my bowels or bladder wanted to spit out. That was a trick I had learned, when there was a toilet and toilet paper you always made good of it. You never knew where you would be when the urge took ahold of you next. I was still sitting there when Moses burst in.

"I told you 10-minutes!" He said through gritted teeth as he grabbed my arm and began dragging me to the kitchen. I was trying to keep up and pull up my underwear and pants as he kept a steady pace.

"S..Sorry." I stammered as he continued through the kitchen and out the front door. The sun was blinding, I hadn't been outside during the day in at least a week. The sun felt warm as it kissed my skin. I turned my face up to it, oblivious of the red van Moses was leading us to. It wasn't until he was shoving into the back of it that I thought to ask what was happening.

"You are leaving, you are going to Miami. I will meet you there in two days' time once I get a few things settled. You are not to speak to your driver and he is not to speak to you. When you get there you will do as you are told and keep your mouth shut. If, and I do mean IF there are any problems with you at all I will kill you, I will kill you and then your mother. Do you understand me?"

I nodded my head in understanding as my tears began to flow. Miami was so far away from home, no one would ever find me there.

The ride was uneventful. The driver stopped only for gas and let me use the restroom at a truck stop. I didn't make eye contact with anyone, I didn't cause any trouble, I didn't speak. I would not take the risk of putting my mother's safety in jeopardy. Escaping or attracting attention was not worth the risk. I could never live with myself, in this life or the next, if I knew I had caused something bad to happen to her.

COMFORT

Arriving in Miami I was brought to a hotel right in the middle of downtown. I was brought into a beautiful suite on the 12th floor. There were seven other girls there who all looked to be between the ages of 16 and 25, although in this business looks can be deceiving. We seem to age faster because of the stuff our bodies are put through not to mention our minds. They were two older woman there as well, they instructed me to call them Madam. I still don't know what either one of their names are. Compared to everyone else I had met they seemed nice. They fawned over me, tweezed my eyebrows let me soak in the tub for an hour, brushed and conditioned my hair, and gave me a manicure and pedicure. There were fancy clothes to choose from and pretty jewelry to wear. By the time Moses showed up I looked like a movie star, if you could ignore the black and blues. The madams had makeup to help cover them, so they didn't look nearly as bad as they had when I arrived. I was sitting on one of the little loveseats listening to the other girls chatter about what they were going to do when they struck it rich when Moses walked in. He nodded his head at me and immediately followed the madams into a private room. The madams were twins. Short, plump twins, with graying brown hair and light brown eyes.

Judging by the conversation the other girls were having I was assuming they were getting paid for their services. The thought excited me, because if that was true that would mean I could bank all of my money until I had enough to buy a bus ticket home. I couldn't contain my excitement and interrupted the conversation addressing a redhead was striking green eyes.

"Excuse me, are you saying that you actually get to keep your money, I mean it's actually your money you can do what you want with it?"

"Well the madams put into a bank account for me, they take out their expenses of course, but they have assured me that when they and I have both made $100,000 I will be free to take my money and leave." She said with a breathy laugh as if I was a silly little child.

She may have thought I was silly, but I looked at her incredulously and laughed right back at her.

"You really think they're saving money for you? They're not saving anything, you are out there doing all the work and they're keeping all the money. Why I bet these clothes and jewels aren't even yours, I know I'm new here but I can say with 100% certainty that we have to share these things and if for some reason we were allowed to leave we would not get to take any of these things with us."

"You don't know what you're talking about!" She said with anger. "You are new here and you don't understand how it works."

I could see the doubt lingering in her eyes, deep down she knew the truth, she just wasn't ready to admit it to herself.

Sticking out my hand I tried to put on a nice smile "my name's Anna by the way, what's yours?"

The redhead didn't answer me; she simply whipped her head around and stalked off, probably to go pout somewhere. For someone in the same position I was in she acted pretty high and mighty, then again maybe I was a bit rude.

Before I got a chance to chat with any of the other girls both the madams with Moses in toe came back into the parlor.

"Look alive ladies! We have a full house

tonight."

In a whirlwind of activity all of the girls were suddenly bustling around, fixing their thigh highs and putting on heels. Before I knew what was happening there was a knock at the door. One of the madams opened it taking a bow. Three little Chinese men came in, all smiling from ear to ear as their eyes eagerly scanned the room. They said something to the madam that I couldn't understand, and she graciously answered them in fluent Chinese.

"April, Megan, and Chloe." She said with a snap of her fingers. Three girls hurriedly ran to approach the men and bowed to each of them. The men each took one girl by her arm in turn and they walked out the door. Over the next half hour the knocks kept coming and one by one the girls left. Finally it was just me sitting alone on the same loveseat.

Moses came and sat beside me, placing a hand on my knee. "You look beautiful Anna. The dress suits you."

I was wearing a teal silky dress that was low-cut and fell just above the knee. The madams handpicked it out for me.

"I want you to know that this is a better life for you, there are no basements here, and I brought you here because I care about your well-being." Moses said with a fatherly stare.

I wasn't sure how to feel about what he was saying. I knew he didn't really care about my well-being or he never would've taken me in the first place. This hotel and these women did seem better than the basements I was kept before. I couldn't argue with him on that point.

"If you behave, if you're a good girl and you do what you're told, you won't ever have to go back to dirty houses and dark basements. There won't be any beatings, and you'll have all the nice dresses and jewelry that you desire." Moses continued.

It definitely did sound like a better life, but better than what? The life that Moses had given me so far or my life that he'd ripped me from? I knew though, that no matter what, I did not want to go back to the basement.

Nodding my head I said to him "of course I will behave, thank you for bringing me here."

"Now there is somebody very special coming to see you tonight, he will expect you to smile and be happy and make small talk with him. He will be very upset if you are unhappy. That would cause problems. Do you understand what I'm trying to say?" Moses asked.

"Yes, I completely understand. Don't worry I won't cause any problems."

Moses smiled at me and leaned in to give me a kiss on the cheek. I managed not to cringe and even gave him a warm smile in return.

"Now we are going to take a little ride, and I will drop you off at his house, I will be waiting just down the block and when the time is up I will pick you back up. You do not speak to him of how you got to be here and you don't say anything about me." He said standing up.

"Yes sir." I answered standing up to follow him out the door.

Outside the hotel there was a town car waiting. Moses acted like a real gentleman even opening the door for me. We drove out of the city and eventually followed a winding driveway up to a set of iron gates. Moses roll down the back window and pushed the call button. Without anybody saying a word the gates sprang to life and began to open. I could feel my stomach began to squirm inside, I was very nervous about what I was getting myself into.

The town car pulled around a circular driveway in front of the front doors. Moses instructed me to get out of the car.

"In three hours we will be parked right back here, you may meet us outside."

I nodded that I understood his instructions,

and stepped out of the car. I was slowly approaching the doors when one of them opened and an older gentleman stepped out. He had a full thick head of salt-and-pepper hair. He was wearing tan slacks and a red polo shirt. He looked like he was in his 50s, but he had a very kind face.

"Anna my dear, you look very lovely this evening. Please, please come in." He said stepping back and allowing me room to walk through the door.

The action reminded me of showing up at the house for the party when Moses tricked me. The flashbacks of that day made me again question what I was getting myself into. Taking a deep breath I knew I didn't have any options though, I put on an award-winning smile and walked through the door hearing it shut with a terrifying click behind me.

BRANDY SULLIVAN

ENOUGH

The next three weeks passed by like a whirlwind. The only client I had to service was the man with the salt-and-pepper hair. That first night at his house he didn't ask for anything other than my company for dinner. I'm not sure exactly what he does for work, it has something to do with stocks and bonds. His phone rings at all hours and he's polite and cordial to all his clients no matter what time of night it is that they call him.

His name is Greg, he used to have a wife but she passed away in a tragic car accident 10 years ago. He doesn't understand why a sweet girl like me would go into the escort service, of course I can't tell him that I was kidnapped and that this life wasn't my choice, Moses would freak and God only knows what would happen to me. I concocted a story about my own parents dying on my 18th birthday. Greg thinks

I'm 19 now. I told him that my parents didn't have life insurance and I became deeply in debt after their death and so being an escort was the quickest way for me to make money to dig myself out of that debt. He believed the story hook line and sinker and even treated me better because of it. He seemed to genuinely feel sorry for me.

The madams were extremely happy when they found out how sorry for me he was. Apparently he started paying extra for me, assuming that I was actually getting the money he turned over to the greedy broads. He wanted me to be able to pay off my debt and get out of this business sooner rather than later. I of course never saw a dime of the money, but I couldn't tell him that either.

He started sending for me three times a week. After the first two times things got physical. He was so old that you would think it would've been impossible for me to act happy and excited about it, but he was also so kind to me that I felt as if I was just paying him back for his kindness.

He took me to plays at the theater, I had never been to the theater before, and I truly enjoyed it. He brought me to fancy restaurants and one night he even surprised me with a private masseuse at his house. It felt like Christmas with him, he was always so full of surprises, and he made it easy for me to imagine that I was living this happy life with him by choice.

We were sitting in his dining room having a candlelight dinner of shrimp scampi one night when the biggest surprise of all came.

"Anna are you happy with me?" Greg asked. His green eyes were shining.

Twirling my hair I gave him my biggest smile "of course I'm happy with you Greg, you're the sweetest most kindest man I ever met."

"What I mean to say, well if I was to ask you, what I want to know is if you would consider moving in with me. The madams explained to me the you have a rather large debt with them as well. I was thinking that if I paid off your debt to them, and any debts that you have back home you would be free to quit the business and move in here, with me, as my wife."

My jaw dropped and I started to weep. I couldn't believe the kindness of this man, I couldn't believe how big his heart was. He was so much different than the parade of men who used to come to use and abuse me. I knew I couldn't tell him yes. Moses would never sell me to him for fear of me opening my mouth and spilling all the gory details of how I really came to be an escort. Greg mistook my tears for sadness.

"Anna, I know I'm old, but I am hoping the you hold a place for me in your heart as I have come to hold a place in mine for you."

"Greg it's not that I don't care for you. I've never met somebody like you before. You're so generous and caring and I know you would never hurt me. Give me some time to think about it, could you do that for me please?"

Even as I said it I knew that all the time in the world wouldn't allow me to give him the answer that he wanted. I just needed to buy some time so that I could tell Moses what was going on. I knew this would mean that I probably wouldn't get to see Greg again, but I wasn't willing to risk the more comfortable life with the madams. I knew if Greg really started pushing that Moses would whisk me away out of here and I couldn't take the chance of being back in the basement or worse.

Greg was still smiling at me, but I could see his sadness in his eyes. I think deep down he knew that I wasn't in going to be able to tell him yes. "Of course Anna. Whatever you wish. Let's retire to the bedroom for the night and we will discuss these matters later."

The next morning my whole world came crashing down. I was sound asleep in bed with two other girls in the suite at the hotel room when Moses came bursting through the door.

"Anna get up right this instant and explain yourself!" Moses screamed at me as I crawled out of bed.

I assumed he was furious about Greg. I figured Greg called the madams with the proposal. I felt my heart lurch up into my throat as I tried to think of a way to explain.

"Is it true that you haven't had to ask the madams for any type of feminine products since you have been here?"

I was so confused, why was Moses asking me about feminine products? I felt a moment of relief when I realized it didn't have anything to do with Greg.

"Get your ass to the bathroom now!" Moses continued to shout.

I hurried into the bathroom and stood near the toilet. Moses slammed the door shut and began to pace.

"You stupid or something? You should've said something! Why? Why is it that I give you a better life than most of the girls and you still insist on screwing up?"

The more Moses ranted the more confused I became. The word feminine products kept flashing in my brain and finally it dawned on me. I put both hands to my stomach without even thinking.

"Do you, I mean..... Am I pregnant?" I asked.

"Are you pregnant? Of course you are pregnant! You shouldn't need me to tell you that. This is a horrible situation and it needs to be taken care of right now."

Before I even had a chance to comprehend what taking care of the situation meant Moses had filled the gap between us and pinned me up against the wall. His fists were like sledgehammers pounding into my stomach over and over again. The pain was unbearable and if it wasn't for the speed of his punches holding me up I would've crumpled on the floor. He continued to beat me until the cramps came over me and I felt the moisture between my legs. Satisfied he had taken care of the situation he simply left me there and walked away.

The pain was unbearable, I couldn't even get up. At some point I must've blacked out. I woke up to one of the girls helping me into the warm tub to clean me up. I just continued to weep, I didn't even acknowledge that she was there or thank her for the help. It's not that I would've wanted the baby, but somehow that attack was more vicious and de-humanizing then the rest. I know I need to find a way out now. I've been writing all this down in hopes that I can get it to somebody before anyone finds it. I can't do this anymore, I can't pretend, I don't even want to see Greg. Regardless of how nice he seems to me he is still after all just another man paying for a prostitute.

If I never get to see my family again the only thing I want them to know is that I love them am thankful for the many happy days they provided in my life. I think back to when my mom would ground me for silly things and I would swear to myself that I hated her. It all seems so stupid to me, so unimportant and childish. I should've cherished those days more and understood that she was just looking out for my safety.

I am sorry, so so very sorry.

Please forgive me, and please help the other girls.

BRANDY SULLIVAN

MARK

Mark sat staring at the last page, completely horrified not only over what he had read, but also of his actions at the police station earlier. He could only hope that Anna was still at the hotel, the hotel that was right across from the Starbucks he met her at. If she was there, and if there were other girls there, the police could just bust in and save them all.

Mark rushed out the door and drove as fast as he could back to the station. Running through the doors the same officer was standing kind of counter.

"Ma'am! Ma'am my name is Mark, I'm sorry but I was in here earlier and I dropped off some papers.."

"Sir if you could just have a seat over there a detective will be right with you." The officer responded before picking up the phone to call whatever detective it was that was going to help him. Judging by her actions Mark could only assume that somebody had already read the papers. They knew about Anna. He felt a sense of relief sweep over him.

He was sitting in the chair with a big sappy grin on his face, happy that something was being done, when a detective in plainclothes approached him.

"Sir am I to assume that you're the one who brought the diary in?"

"Yes, I did and look I am sorry that I just dropped it and ran. I just didn't want to get involved in anything."

"My name is detective Anderson. What I am at liberty to tell you at this time is that we have some of our finest officers as well as SWAT team at the hotel now. What I would like to know is where you got this diary from?"

Mark relayed the events that happened that fateful morning at Starbucks. The detective verified the address of the Starbucks Mark was talking about and came to the conclusion that they had the right hotel. Apparently there had been some reports of a lot of activity and people coming and going from that particular suite. The diary gave them the information they needed to obtain a search warrant.

Feeling relieved Mark asked him if he could wait around long enough to hear the results.

"I'm really concerned about Anna, and I am hoping that she is okay." Mark explained to him.

"So you read the diary I am assuming?"

"Yes sir." Mark said "I couldn't help it sir, some strange woman hands you something your curiosity takes over."

"I fully understand. You may wait here. There's a soda machine and restrooms down the hall. When the officers get back, if they have Anna with them, you are not to interfere in our investigation. We will ask her if she would like to speak with you. Until you are instructed to do so you do not speak to anybody that we bring back. We truly appreciate you turning the papers into this department, but you cannot interfere with this investigation." The detective said before walking away.

He didn't even give Mark a chance to respond and although Mark thought he was being a bit short with him he was still elated that somebody was doing something. He sat in his chair for two hours waiting for news. Mark knew something was up when he found numerous officers gathering in the front lobby.

He kept his eyes fixed on the main doors as other officers walked in, some of them holding the arms of people in handcuffs. There were two men handcuffed, as well as two middle-aged woman. Mark couldn't help but jump up out of his seat when he noticed the next people coming in were younger girls, also in handcuffs. One of these girls was Anna. She was staring at the floor with tears streaming down her face as the officer led her by her elbow.

"Anna! Anna is that you?" Mark yelled.

She turned her head and Mark saw the spark of recognition her eyes. She gave him a small weak smile as she was led to the back where he presumed the holding cells were. Mark didn't leave, he sat back down and took up vigil in the same seat he had been sitting in throughout the evening. No matter how many officers he asked or how many times he bothered them, nobody would tell him anything. It was three hours later by the time Mark got any news.

A woman in plain clothes came out and approached Mark. "Sir, Anna would like to see you if you are up for it." She said to him.

"Yes, yes I am up for it. Where is she?"

"Right this way sir."

ANNA...AFTERMATH

If this was a fairytale I would tell you that when Mark broke through the doors of the holding cell I threw my arms around him and hugged him for being my Savior. That we fell in love, got married, had kids, and lived happily ever after.

If this was a fairytale...

What really happened was that Mark came in, sat down, and other than a few polite "are you okay? and thank you's" we found we didn't have a lot to say to each other. Mark knew me from what he had read in the pages that I gave him, I knew him as the man who brought those pages to the police department. As happy as he was to know that I was alive, he also seemed very uncomfortable around me. When I did hug him I felt him fight the urge to pull away from me, as if I was some tainted and dirty thing. I can't say that's how he felt, I can only say it's the way I feel he felt.

My family all arrived in Miami within 24 hours of them being notified. They also seemed uncomfortable and awkward around me after the officers filled them in on my ordeal. I could tell the relief for my safety and the fact that I was alive were genuine, but I could also tell that they didn't know how to feel about the things I had done. It didn't matter that I was forced to do them. I don't blame them for feeling that way, there is no way they're supposed to feel. I don't even know how I'm supposed to feel. There are some days I look in the mirror and feel disgust for myself. There are days where I question whether I should've just let them kill me.

I was unable to leave Miami for a while. At first the officers wanted to charge me for prostitution. When they decided not to and decided that I really was a victim they wanted me to testify at the trial against the madams and Moses. I adamantly refused and finally somebody from victim services came and took my sworn statement and said that that would be good.

I bare scars from both my physical and emotional wounds. These scars now affect my everyday life. I am suspicious of everybody, I get nervous when men approached me, and even though I have now been therapy for over a year I don't feel like it has helped. I had to have a full physical examination after the bust on the hotel was made. I found out I was in fact pregnant, and the Moses of beating had led to a miscarriage. I also found out that I had gonorrhea.

The doctor started me on a range of medications to cover STDs, and vitamins to cover the malnutrition, and sleeping pills to keep the nightmares at bay. I'm still on the sleeping pills and mood stabilizers. I am living at home with my parents and am currently taking GED classes online. What happened to me was all over the local papers when I first came home and I knew I would not be able to handle going back to high school and facing the stares from people who would never understand. I have connected with other survivors online, my mother things that this just keeps all the wounds fresh for me and that I shouldn't talk to them, but for me it's a way to get my feelings off my chest with people who do understand, and people who I know our secretly judging me behind their looks of pity.

Sharing my story with the world will hopefully help open its eyes to the reality that this kind of thing is happening all around them. Lonely men look for escort services, strip clubs, brothels, or prostitutes walking the streets. Quite a few of them are seeking woman who they believe are willingly out there doing this stuff to make a quick buck. What they don't realize is that many of these women are victims, many of them are doing these things out of fear and against their will. I know I will never look at a prostitute the same way again. Instead of looking upon them with disgust and hate I will look upon them with concern and pity.

Facts

And

Information

on

Trafficking

BRANDY SULLIVAN

How does human trafficking take place?

While not true for all victims, traffickers normally target people in developing countries where poverty is rampant. This is normally done through some means of force or deception and the victims are typically extremely young. Most victims range in age from 8 to 18 years old. With this in mind, it should be noted that traffickers have been known to take people as young as four or five years old.

The deception is the key part to snagging a victim; normally a trafficker will target somebody who's looking for a better life. They may approach a young girl and offer her a job as a server, a dancer, or housemaid in a foreign wealthy country. Some of these wealthy countries included the United States, Great Britain, and Italy.

It is not until the victim arrives at their destination that the traffickers take away their passports, and normally as a way to make them more submissive the trafficker will either physically or sexually abuse the victim. Oftentimes females are forced into prostitution in the foreign country where the victim neither speaks the language nor has any means of support.

A trafficking victim is commonly forced to serve up to 8 to 15 clients a day, and they do not receive any actual pay. The traffickers will tell them that any money made is being used to pay off their debt. The trafficker will tell them that they owe debt for transportation, food, lodging, and whatever else they feel it coming up with as an excuse.

When the trafficker is sick of this particular victim they will oftentimes sell them to another trafficker. It becomes a viscous and hopeless circle. The new trafficker informs the victim that they have to start paying off their new debt. A trafficking victim is at high risk for acquiring AIDS, hepatitis, and unwanted pregnancies. The traffickers do not take care to get their victims professional medical help and so unwanted pregnancies are dealt with in gruesome ways. The victim has a much higher chance of dying in an early age and for some of them they long for death as a way to escape their horrible existence.

The Internet and Trafficking

In the United States the Internet is the number one place for the buying and selling of woman and children for sex. Two major sites that play and have played a large role in trafficking are craigslist and Backpage.com. In 2011 it is estimated that Backpage.com Brian and annual revenue of over $20 million from human trafficking. $20 million of slave money. Craigslist and the other sites rake in millions every year for sex ads. It should be noted that craigslist did take steps to try to reduce the number of under aged trafficking ads on the Internet. People simply moved their ads from the adult services section to the casual encounters and therapeutic services sections. Ads can be disguised as masseuse ads or people looking for someone to just hang out with. There is no actual mention of sex, but people who troll these websites know what the lingo means.

Backpage.com has become the number one place for sex ads online. The company itself rakes in over $17 million a year for the ads. The only silver lining to these websites aiding in human trafficking industry is that they can be tracked by investigators.

County Sheriff's Department in Florida was able to

successfully accomplish the craigslist sting. The sting included 15 alleged child predators. Total number of arrests made in that sting were 44 and according to reports the sex ring did business on craigslist and back page.

The owners and moderators of these sites need to wake up and open their eyes. By choosing to allow the ads to be posted and turning their heads they are in fact helping facilitate the sale of woman and children.

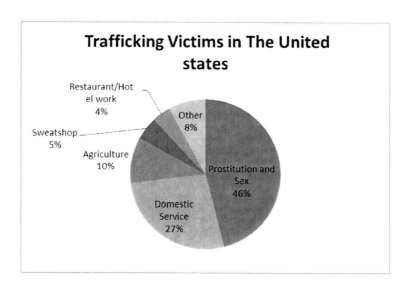

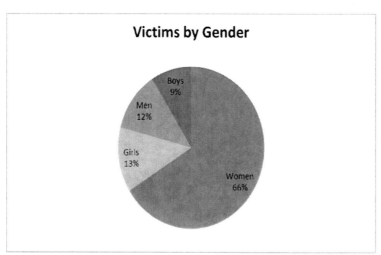

BRANDY SULLIVAN

Myth Vs. Fact

Myth: trafficked persons can only be foreign nationals or are only immigrants from other countries.
Reality: Human trafficking encompasses both transnational trafficking that crosses borders and domestic or internal trafficking that occurs within a country.
Myth : Human trafficking is the same as human smuggling.
Reality: There are many differences between these crimes. Both are entirely separate Federal crimes in the United States. Most notably, smuggling is a crime against a country's borders, whereas human trafficking is a crime against a person.

Myth : Sex trafficking is the only form of human trafficking.
Reality: Elements of human trafficking can occur in the commercial sex industry as well as in situations of forced labor or services. Human trafficking encompasses both "sex trafficking" and "labor trafficking," and can affect men and women, children and adults.

Estimated number of slaves in the world today:

10-30 Million

BRANDY SULLIVAN

Resources:

☐ End Slavery Now www.endslaverynow.com

☐ Free the Slaves www.freetheslaves.net
☐ Global Initiative to Fight Trafficking www.ungift.org

☐ International Justice Mission www.ijm.org

☐ Not For Sale www.notforsalecampaign.org

☐ Polaris Project www.polarisproject.org

☐ Shared Hope International www.sharedhope.org

☐ Blue Heart Campaign www.unodc.org/blueheart

☐ Coalition Against Trafficking in Women www.catwinternational.org

☐ ECPAT-USAwww.ecpatusa.org

BRANDY SULLIVAN

ABOUT THE AUTHOR

Brandy Sullivan lives in Vermont, with her husband and four children. Writing about important issues has always been a passion of hers. When she is not writing she is spending time in the kitchen baking or practicing her acrylic painting skills.

www.facebook.com/BrandySullivanAuthor

BRANDY SULLIVAN

CPSIA information can be obtained
at www.ICGtesting.com
Printed in the USA
LVOW11s1631051116

511780LV00001B/112/P